A Day in the Life of A Dollar Bill

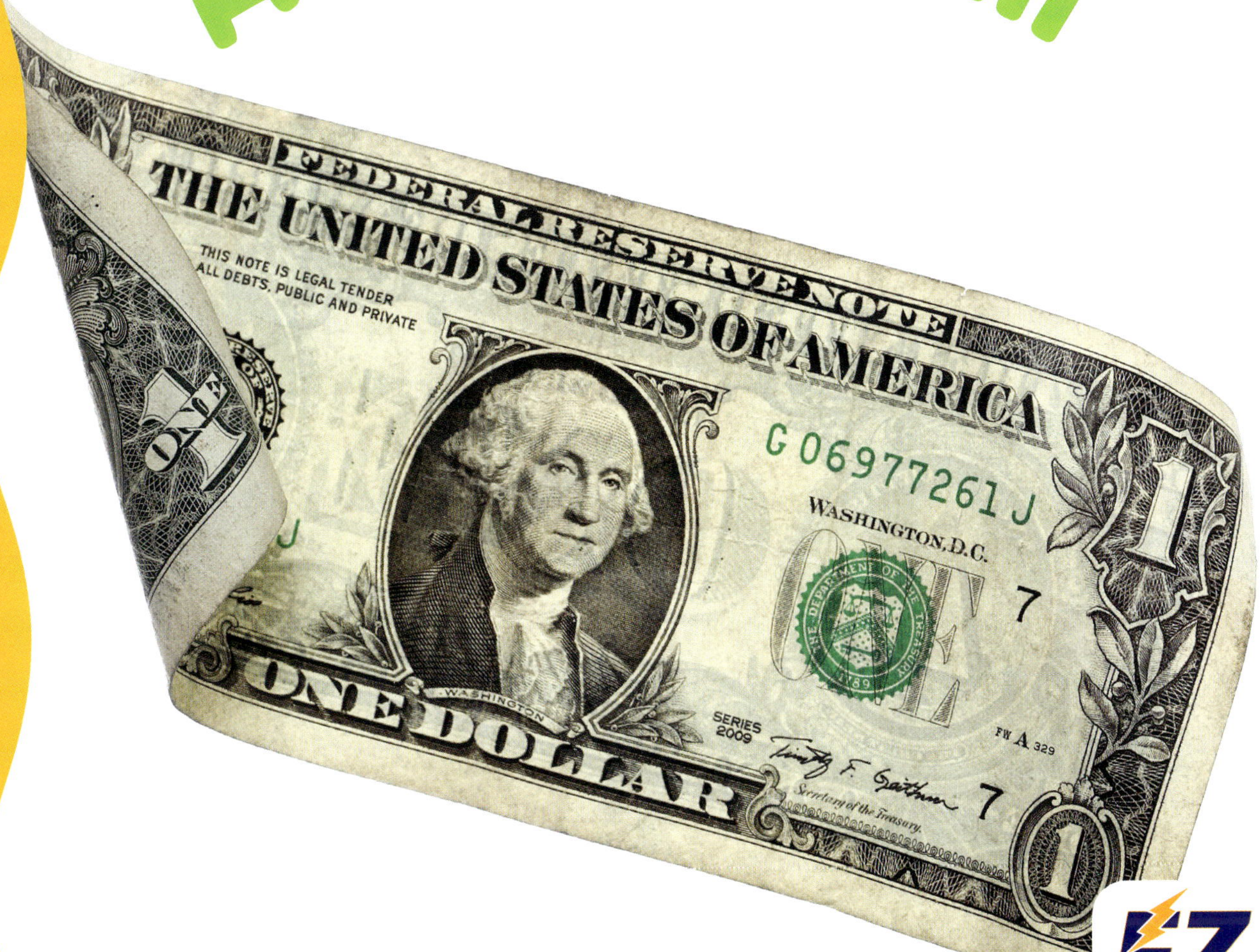

Meg Greve

EZ READERS
AN IMPRINT OF
MITCHELL LANE PUBLISHERS

CREATING YOUNG NONFICTION READERS

EZ Readers offer nonfiction for beginning readers in PreK through first grade, using simple language, clear illustrations, and engaging facts to build vocabulary and confidence.

TIPS FOR READING NONFICTION WITH BEGINNING READERS

Talk about Nonfiction

Begin by explaining that nonfiction books give us information that is true. The book will be organized around a specific topic or idea, and we may learn new facts through reading.

Look at the Parts

Most nonfiction books have helpful features. Our *EZ Readers* include color photographs and graphic aids, a table of contents, a glossary, and an index. Share the purpose of these features with your reader.

Color Photos and Graphic Aids

A lot of information can be found by "reading" photos, charts, maps, and other graphic aids found within nonfiction texts. Help your reader learn more about the different ways information can be displayed.

Table of Contents

Located at the front of the book, this list shows the big ideas within the text and the page numbers where they can be found.

Glossary

Located at the back of the book, the glossary defines key words and phrases that are related to the topic. These words and phrases can be found in the text in colored type.

Index

Located at the back of the book, an index is an alphabetical list of topics and the page numbers where they can be found.

With a little help and guidance about reading nonfiction, you can feel good about introducing a young reader to the world of *EZ Readers* nonfiction books.

EZ Readers is an imprint of:

Mitchell Lane
PUBLISHERS

2001 SW 31st Avenue
Hallandale, FL 33009
mitchelllanepub.com

First Edition, 2027.

Author: Meg Greve
Designer: Rhea Magaro
Editor: Kim Thompson

Library of Congress Cataloging-in-Publication Data
Title: A Day in the Life of a Dollar Bill / by Meg Greve

Description: Hallandale, FL :
Mitchell Lane Publishers, [2027]

Identifiers:
ISBN 979-8-89260-846-6 (library bound)
ISBN 979-8-89260-936-4 (eBook)

Library of Congress Control Number: 2025950834

PHOTO CREDITS
Shutterstock: xpixel, 1; Ruslan Lytvyn, 5; Mega Pixel, 5; Rawpixel.com, 7, 22; graja, 8; nizammg, 9; Kittyfly, 10, 22; Mr.Louis, 13, 22; glenda, 14, 22; Pixel-Shot, 17, 22; AnnaStills, 18, 22; New Africa, 21; refrina, 22; SherryArts, 22.

Table of Contents

I Am a Dollar Bill

I am made of strong paper.

I am the same as 10 dimes.

I am the same as
four **quarters**.

BY THE WAY...

George Washington is on me. He was America's first president.

You did a **chore**. (Good job!)

You got paid two dollars.

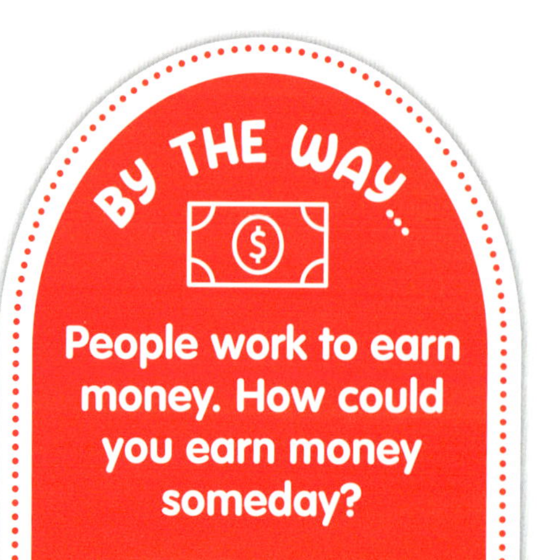

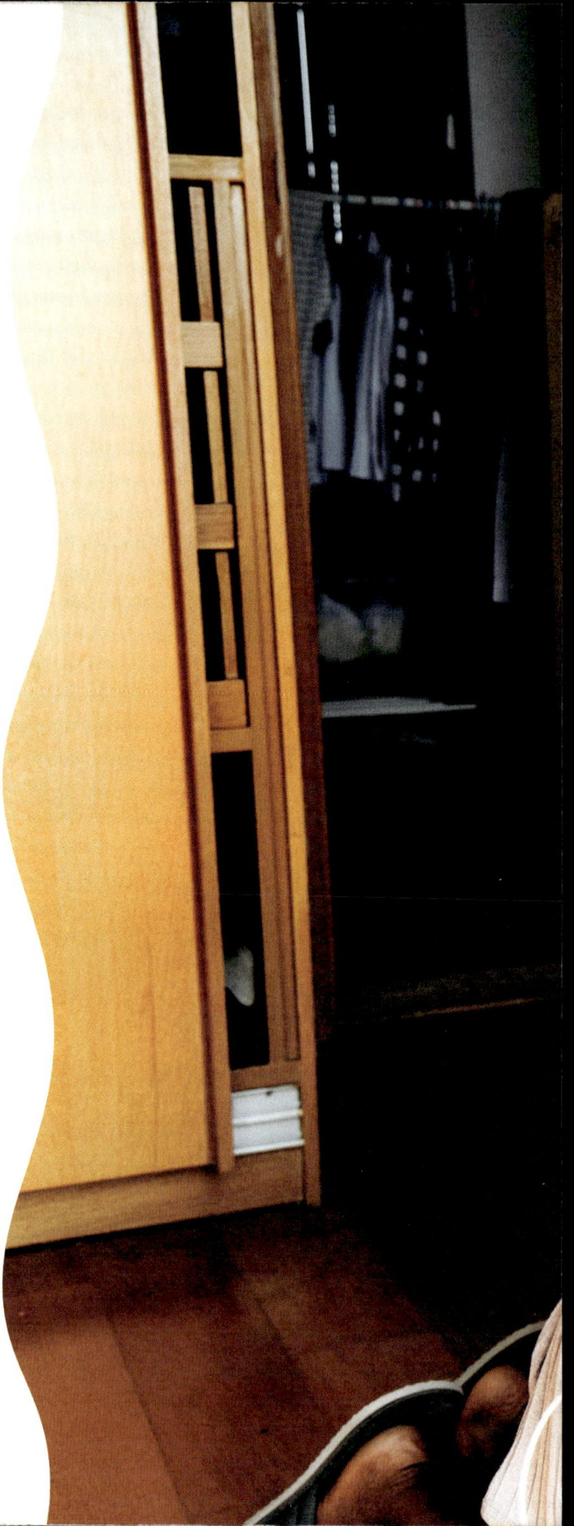

Easy-Care
Off
Cottons/Coloureds
Extra Dry
Cupboard Dry Plus
Cupboard Dry
Iron Dry
Woollen Finish
Rapid
Programme time

THINK ABOUT IT...

Why is it good to save some of your money?
Why is it good to share some of your money with others?

You saved one dollar bill.

You will spend one dollar bill.
(That is me!)

BY THE WAY...

Do not lose me! I am also safe in a purse or a pocket.

I go into your **wallet**.
(It is cozy in here.)

I am excited to take a trip!

I help you buy something at the **store**.

I go into the **cash register**. (Wheee!)

BY THE WAY...
Goodbye! I may see you again someday!

A man buys something.

I am his **change**.

I go into his hand.

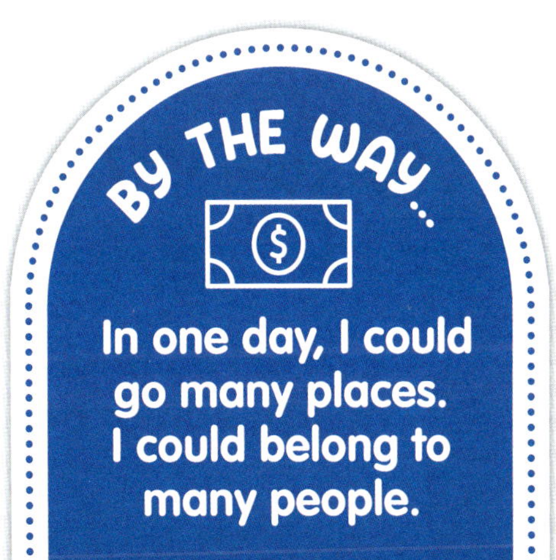

The man sees a **stand**.

He buys lemonade.

He pays with me!

LEMONADE
250 ml - 30¢
350 ml - 50¢
TASTY
LEMONADE
50¢

A kid counts me.

He takes me to the **bank**.

I feel safe here.

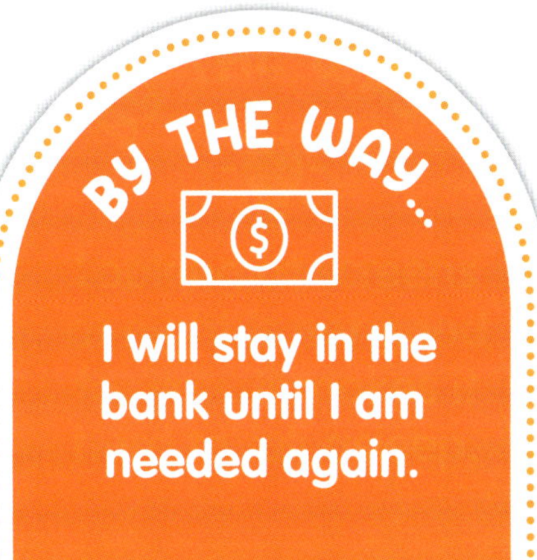

Do you get the *cents* that money is important?

(See? I made a joke!)

I am proud to do my job.

I help you buy what you need and want.

Glossary

bank (bangk) a place where money is kept; when people use debit cards, the money comes out of the bank

cash register (kash REJ-i-stur) a machine that is used in stores to keep track of purchases and that has a drawer for cash

change (chaynj) the money you get back if you pay more than something costs

chore (chor) a job that must be done regularly, such as cleaning or mowing the grass

quarters (KWOR-turz) coins worth 25 cents or one-quarter of a dollar

stand (stand) a small booth, counter, or stall where things are sold

store (stor) a building where things are sold

wallet (WAH-lit) a small, flat case for holding money